XTREME RAPTORS

★ ★ ★ ★

RAPTOR RESCUE

BY

JOHN HAMILTON

A&D Xtreme
An imprint of Abdo Publishing | abdopublishing.com

abdopublishing.com

Published by Abdo Publishing, a division of ABDO, PO Box 398166, Minneapolis, Minnesota 55439. Copyright ©2018 by Abdo Consulting Group, Inc. International copyrights reserved in all countries. No part of this book may be reproduced in any form without written permission from the publisher. A&D Xtreme™ is a trademark and logo of Abdo Publishing.

Printed in the United States of America, North Mankato, Minnesota.
032017
052017

THIS BOOK CONTAINS
RECYCLED MATERIALS

Editor & Graphic Design: Sue Hamilton
Cover Design: Candice Keimig
Cover Photo: iStock
Interior Photos: Alamy-pgs 10-11 & 16-17; AP-pgs 2-3, 4-5, 20-21, 24 & 26-27; Ardea-pg 6; AlaskaStock-pg 9; Billi West/Clay County Sheriff's Office-pg 8; Getty-pgs 12, 14, 15, 18-19 & 22-23; John Hamilton-pgs 1 & 28-32; The Raptor Center/University of Minnesota-pg 7 (top); Washington State University College of Veterinary Medicine-pgs 13 & 25; Wildlife Center of Virginia-pg 7 (x-ray).

Websites
To learn more about Raptors, visit abdobooklinks.com. These links are routinely monitored and updated to provide the most current information available.

Publisher's Cataloging-in-Publication Data
Names: Hamilton, John, author.
Title: Raptor rescue / by John Hamilton.
Description: Minneapolis, MN : Abdo Publishing, 2018. |
Series: Xtreme raptors
     Includes index.
Identifiers: LCCN 2016962221 |
ISBN 9781532110061 (lib. bdg.) |
     ISBN 9781680787917 (ebook)
Subjects: LCSH: Birds of prey--Juvenile literature. |
Wildlife rescue--Juvenile literature.
Classification: DDC 598.9--dc23
LC record available at http://lccn.loc.gov/2016962221

CONTENTS

RAPTOR CENTERS

Raptors are fierce birds of prey. Their large eyes help them spot fish or small animals from afar. They grip and kill their prey with their strong feet and sharp talons. Their hooked beaks help them tear off small chunks of flesh they can swallow.

But raptors do have accidents. Sometimes they get injured so badly they need to be rescued. That is when the veterinarians and volunteers at raptor centers are called to action.

A vet inspects and treats a barn owl *(Tyto alba)* with a broken wing at the Wildlife Rehabilitation Rescue Centre in Stara Zagora, Bulgaria.

INJURIES

Raptors and their environment are much healthier today than they were 50 years ago. Air and water pollution are greatly reduced. Laws today forbid the use of many poisons and pesticides, such as DDT, that were once commonplace.

A peregrine falcon *(Falco peregrinus)* nest shows the effects of DDT on bird eggs. The too-thin eggshells easily cracked under the parent's weight. DDT was banned in 1972.

XTREME FACT – "Healthy raptors, healthy world" means that when raptor populations are healthy, it's a good sign that the environment also is healthy.

However, many hazards continue to threaten raptors. For example, hundreds of bald eagles and other raptors each year are sickened after eating carrion contaminated with lead. In the United States alone, hunters using lead ammunition release 8,000 to 10,000 tons (7,257 to 9,072 metric tons) of the toxin into the environment each year.

A bald eagle *(Haliaeetus leucocephalus)* with lead poisoning at a raptor rescue site. It can no longer lift itself up.

A bald eagle's x-ray shows lead shot in the raptor's stomach. Untreated, an eagle will die within 2 to 3 weeks after swallowing lead.

THE WILDLIFE CENTER OF VA
WAYNESBORO VA

Besides poison and sickness, raptors face other hazards. Many are caused by human activity. Raptor centers often treat birds that have flown into glass windows, moving vehicles, or electrical power lines.

A bald eagle is trapped in the front grille of a car. Because eagles eat carrion, such as animals killed on roadways, the raptors are frequently struck by vehicles. This eagle was carefully removed and survived.

XTREME FACT – At the University of Minnesota's Raptor Center, the most common species of injured birds include bald eagles, red-tailed hawks, great horned owls, and kestrels.

Other dangers include steel-jaw traps, fishing lines and hooks, or being shot by hunters. (It is against the law to kill or capture raptors.) There are also many natural hazards. They include being stuck in mud or falling from nests.

A bald eagle with a fishhook in its mouth.

EXAMS & TESTS

Raptor centers are similar to hospital emergency rooms. When an injured bird first arrives, exams and tests are performed right away. Vets and trained helpers examine the raptor, checking its talons, wings, feathers, eyes, and beak.

An injured white-bellied sea eagle *(Haliaeetus leucogaster)* is examined.

A seriously injured raptor is immediately taken to a critical care room. The bird can be given intravenous (IV) fluids and oxygen while veterinarians try to save its life.

 XTREME FACT – Injured birds are brought to the raptor center by staff member experts, volunteers, or concerned citizens.

Raptors, like very young children, cannot tell people what is wrong with them. Veterinarians search for clues by giving the birds thorough exams. If raptors are covered in dirt, mud, or oil, they must be washed.

An oil-covered bald eagle sits in a carrier waiting to be washed.

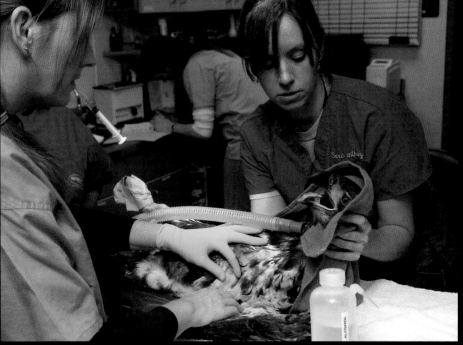

A young bald eagle is cared for by vets at the College of Veterinary Medicine at Washington State University in Pullman, Washington.

Raptors do not understand that humans are trying to help them. They must be held down. Staff members wear thick gloves to protect against sharp talons and beaks. Raptors are often wrapped in soft blankets, with a hood covering their head, to help keep them calm.

XTREME FACT – In many cases, raptors are so badly injured that they cannot be saved and must be humanely euthanized.

Raptors are weighed and checked for overall health. That includes taking their pulse and blood pressure. Veterinarians look for cuts or broken bones. Blood tests are often needed to pinpoint why a raptor is sick.

A veterinarian draws blood from the leg of a scared and wounded black kite *(Milvus migrans)* at the Wild Animal Clinic in Israel.

 XTREME FACT – Some raptor centers have advanced diagnostic equipment. Endoscopes are often used to treat throat and lung ailments. Electrocardiograms (EKGs) monitor the heart.

A vet puts a great horned owl *(Bubo virginianus)* to sleep to treat its injuries at The Wildlife Center of Virginia in Waynesboro, Virginia.

Broken wing bones are a common injury. When x-rays are required, the bird is put to sleep with a special gas to keep it still. The gas is given by placing a hood over the raptor's head. Gas travels through a tube connected to the hood.

Surgery & Treatment

If vets believe an injured raptor can be saved, surgery is sometimes performed. Fishhooks are removed, along with lead fishing sinkers that may have been swallowed.

A vet operates on a bald eagle that was shot. It is illegal in the United States to harm raptors. A person found guilty of shooting a raptor faces a $5,000 fine or a year in prison.

Gunshot wounds are cleaned and bandaged. Antibiotics are applied to make sure germs do not spread. If a raptor has been electrocuted, such as by flying into a high-voltage power line, special care must be taken because of damaged feathers and the chance of infection.

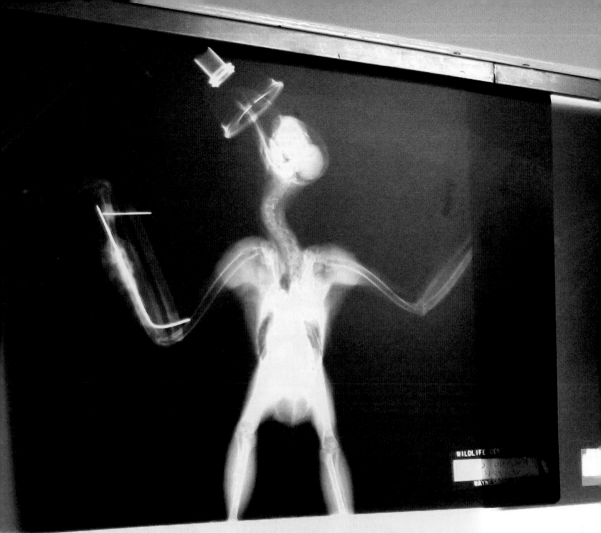

Some raptor centers specialize in fixing broken bones. The most common fractures are in wing or leg bones. X-rays are used to help veterinarians locate and fix fractures. Metal and plastic rods are placed in the bones. Stainless steel wire also helps stabilize the bones and help them heal.

A veterinarian from The Wildlife Center of Virginia compares before- and after-surgery x-rays of a bird with a broken wing.

XTREME FACT – *It is important to stabilize broken bones as soon as possible. Bird bones have high mineral content, which results in sharp fractures. These sharp edges can easily damage blood vessels, nerves, or muscles.*

RECOVERY

Raptors spend weeks or even months recovering from their injuries or sicknesses. Birds that have been exposed to toxins need special care. Common toxins include pesticides, oil, mercury, and lead.

A bald eagle is tube-fed water to keep it hydrated.

Treatment includes special antidote drugs, pain medication, intravenous (IV) fluids, and rest. Raptors that suffer lung damage are sometimes placed in intensive care cages. The incubator units provide extra oxygen, heat, and humidity to help the birds heal faster.

XTREME FACT – *Almost one-third of bald eagles brought to raptor centers suffer from the toxic effects of lead poisoning. They most commonly ingest lead bullet fragments after eating a deer carcass or gut pile that has been left behind by hunters. Hunters can eliminate this threat to raptors by using copper bullets instead of lead.*

Raptors are like the professional athletes of the avian world. In the wild, they need to be in top physical condition to catch prey and survive. When they are injured, they require rest, medicine, and physical therapy to get back into shape. Broken bones take up to six weeks to completely heal.

XTREME FACT – *Recovering birds are fed a whole-animal diet, usually mice, rats, quail, or fish. Prey animals are either prepared or freshly killed. Providing whole animals ensures raptors get proper nutrition.*

Raptors are kept in quiet rooms or pet carriers as they recover. They are given medicine and food to keep their strength up.

An injured Cape vulture (*Gyps coprotheres*) recovers at the VulPro Vulture Rehabilitation Centre in South Africa.

A barn owl grows stronger as it moves inside its cage. The recovering raptor is part of the Second Chances Wildlife Rehabilitation Program at the Texas State Aquarium in Corpus Christi, Texas.

After casts and bandages are removed, recovering raptors are placed in larger pens. This lets them fly short distances to strengthen their wing muscles. They begin to hunt live food placed in the pens.

Eventually, raptors are taken outdoors. They get regular exercise while attached to long tethers. Volunteers and raptor center staff chart the birds' progress. Most raptor patients need about three to four months before they are ready to be released.

A recovering young bald eagle gets tethered exercise. This allows the raptor to build up its strength before it is released back into the wild.

XTREME FACT – *If a raptor survives its first week at a raptor center, it has about a 70 percent chance of fully recovering and being released back into the wild.*

RELEASE

Release day is very special. When raptors are fully recovered, they are taken to wild places suitable for each species. There must be enough prey and habitat in which to survive.

A rehabilitated
red-tailed hawk
(*Buteo jamaicensis*)
is released near
Columbia, Missouri.

Metal bands are placed on the raptors' legs
so they can later be identified. They are then
hoisted into the air and released into the wild.
It is a joyful time for the staff and volunteers
as they watch their former patients take flight
and soar toward a new life.

*XTREME FACT – The University of Minnesota's Raptor
Center treats more than 800 sick and injured wild
raptors on average each year. Of those, about 350
eventually recover and are released.*

OUTREACH

Some raptors can never be released. Their injured wings or talons don't fully heal. They may have become too tame and are unable to hunt. These birds would starve to death in the wild. They remain at the raptor center. Some are sent to other licensed programs.

A speaker from The Raptor Center at the University of Minnesota talks to a crowd at the Minnesota State Fair.

The raptors are used in demonstrations at schools, parks, and county fairs. They help educate the public about raptors and their importance in our world.

This outreach activity helps raptor centers raise much-needed money. More importantly, these bird ambassadors teach people ways to help and protect raptors and their shrinking habitat.

GLOSSARY

CARRION
The dead flesh of animals that are decaying.

DDT
DDT (dichlorodiphenyltrichloroethane) was a chemical product used to kill mosquitoes and other insects in the 1940s and 1950s. It got into water supplies. The chemical caused birds' eggshells to break easily. After this was discovered, DDT use was banned in 1972.

ELECTROCARDIOGRAM
A machine that records the electrical activity of the heart. Certain sicknesses can be detected by analyzing heartbeats.

ENDOSCOPE
A slim, tubular device for peering into body cavities such as throats and stomachs. Endoscopes are most often made with fiber optic material that allows light to pass through. They help diagnose illnesses, as well as assist in surgery.

EUTHANIZE
To kill a creature that is hopelessly sick or injured. It is an act of mercy that is done in a relatively painless way, often by lethal injection.

INTRAVENOUS (IV) FLUIDS

Fluids that are given to sick animals or humans directly through a blood vessel. The fluids can be simple water to keep the creature hydrated, or can contain various medicines. A needle pierces a vein near the skin. A tube is then connected to the needle, and fluids are passed through it directly into the patient.

HABITAT

The natural home of a living thing.

LEAD

A heavy toxic metal that has no safe exposure level in humans or animals. It damages the nervous system and blood. Lead is often used to make bullets. Raptors can get lead poisoning when they eat carrion that has been killed by hunters using lead bullets. The raptors consume the toxic lead fragments along with the meat. Lead poisoning is among the most common causes of death in bald eagles.

SPECIES

A group of plants or animals that are related to one another. They look alike and may produce offspring.

INDEX